LANGUAGE AND MIND

A STUDY GUIDE

William Snyder
University of Connecticut

K∃ KENDALL/HUNT PUBLISHING COMPANY
4050 Westmark Drive   Dubuque, Iowa 52002

Cover images courtesy of Corel

CONTENTS

Unit VI: Language in Exceptional Circumstances 63

INTRODUCTION

This study guide is designed for use in the course *Language and Mind*, offered by the Department of Linguistics at the University of Connecticut. *Language and Mind* is a one-semester, lower-division under-graduate course, in which students attend two plenary lectures and one smaller discussion section each week. The material provided here is intended as a guide to note-taking during the plenary lectures. The hope is to indicate which points are the most important, so that students can focus their attention and note-taking efforts appropriately.

For each lecture a list of key terms and concepts is provided, together with ample space for recording the definitions given during the lecture. In addition, diagrams and examples that are important for the student to remember, but potentially too cumbersome to write down during the lecture, are provided here. Finally, multiple-choice review questions are provided at the end of each unit. The review questions are similar in format and content to the questions normally used on examinations in the course.

UNIT I

THE NATURE OF HUMAN LANGUAGE

SECTION 1

LINGUISTIC SOPHISTICATION AND MATERIAL CULTURE

Informal Questionnaire

Please indicate whether you agree or disagree with each of the following statements:

1. Agree   Disagree   Some of the world's languages are grammatically more complex than others.

2. Agree   Disagree   Parents and other caregivers teach young children their language.

3. Agree   Disagree   Some languages take longer than others for children to learn.

4. Agree   Disagree   Linguistic abilities steadily increase as a child grows older.

5. Agree   Disagree   Formal, careful speech is grammatically more sophisticated than casual, everyday speech.

6. Agree   Disagree   Cultures with greater technological sophistication tend to have grammatically richer languages.

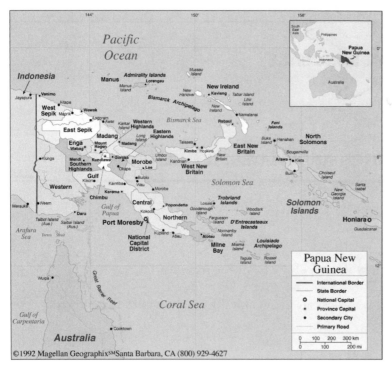

©1992 Magellan Geographix℠Santa Barbara, CA (800) 929-4627

©MAPS.com/CORBIS

CouponCo Worldwide, Inc.

SECTION 2

DESCRIPTION AND PRESCRIPTION

A. Be prepared to define the following key terms:

➤ Prescriptive Grammar —

➤ Descriptive Grammar —

➤ Native Speaker —

➤ Ungrammatical —

➤ The Like-insertion Rule —

B. Quotes for discussion:

Edwin Newman (1980) *On Language.* New York, NY: Warner Books.

Will America be the death of English? (...) My well-thought-out mature judgment is that it will. (p. 3)

Those who wanted to show that they were down to earth, and so not above using Y'know, or — much the same thing — telling you that somebody is like six feet tall, have been particularly influential. (p. 18)

Some people collapse into Y'know after giving up trying to say what they mean. Others scatter it broad-side... (p. 17)

Moon Zappa. Vocals for "Valley Girl," on Frank Zappa's (1982) album, *Ship Arriving Too Late to Save a Drowning Witch.*

Encino is like SO BITCHEN.
There's like the Galleria,
And like all these like really great shoe stores.

U.S. Department of Transportation

SECTION 3

CONSCIOUS KNOWLEDGE AND TACIT KNOWLEDGE

A. Be prepared to define the following key terms:

➤ Competence —

➤ Performance —

➤ Grammaticality Judgement —

➤ Ambiguity —

➤ Wanna Contraction —

➤ Tacit Knowledge —

B. Exercise: (Use your neighbor as a linguistic consultant.)

Grammaticality Judgements: (**OK** or *)

1. ____ I wanna go to a movie. (='I want to go to a movie.')

2. ____ He wanna go to a movie. (='He wants to go to a movie.')

3. ____ Who do you wanna visit Mary? (='Who do you want to visit Mary?')

Ambiguity:

4. Who do you want to visit?
    a. (Answer:) I want John to visit. *Is this a possible answer?* ____
    b. (Answer:) I want to visit John. *Is this a possible answer?* ____

5. Who do you wanna visit?
    a. (Answer:) I want John to visit. *Is this a possible answer?* ____
    b. (Answer:) I want to visit John. *Is this a possible answer?* ____

SECTION 4

THE CREATIVE ASPECT OF HUMAN LANGUAGE

A. Nominal Compounds in English

$$N \longrightarrow N \ N$$ (Note: Rule can apply **recursively**.)

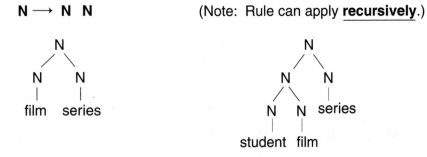

Also: *student film series committee, student film series committee budget report, etc.*

B. Be prepared to define the following key terms:

➤ Hierarchical Structure —

➤ Tree Diagram —

➤ Nominal Compound —

➤ Head —

➤ Right-Hand Head Rule —

➤ Recursion —

SECTION 5

EMPIRICISM AND NATIVISM (OR "WHY LING 101 IS CONTROVERSIAL")

Be prepared to define the following key terms:

➤ Empiricism —

➤ Tabula Rasa —

➤ Nativism —

➤ Innate Knowledge —

➤ Universal Grammar —

11

1. Evidence from languages in New Guinea shows that:
   a. Technological sophistication determines grammatical sophistication.
   b. Grammatical sophistication determines technological sophistication.
   c. Grammatical sophistication is independent of technological sophistication.

2. Evidence from "like" insertion in Valley Talk shows that:
   a. Encino is like so bitchen.
   b. Even casual everyday speech is grammatically sophisticated.
   c. Careful, formal speech is grammatically more sophisticated than everyday speech.

3. The 17th century English writer John Dryden wrote the rule "Do not end a sentence with a preposition." This is an example of:
   a. descriptive grammar.
   b. prescriptive grammar.
   c. universal grammar.

4. Recursion is a property of language that can help us explain how we get:
   a. infinite language from finite means.
   b. finite language from finite means.
   c. finite language from infinite means.

5. Empiricism attempts to explain child language acquisition in terms of:
   a. human biology.
   b. the child's environment.
   c. natural selection.

UNIT II

CHILDREN'S ACQUISITION OF LANGUAGE

SECTION 6

EVIDENCE FOR NATIVISM

A. Characteristics of Language Acquisition

➤ Universality —

➤ Uniformity —

➤ Rapidity —

➤ Consistency of Stages —

➤ Developmental Dissociations —

➤ Creolization —

B. Some Stages of Language Acquisition

➤ Babbling —

➤ Holophrastic Speech —

➤ Telegraphic Speech —

SECTION 7

THE ARGUMENT FROM THE POVERTY OF THE STIMULUS

A. The Argument from the Poverty of the Stimulus

➤ No Explicit Instruction

➤ No (Reliable) Negative Evidence

➤ Cultural Variation in Adult-Child Interactions

➤ Content, Not Grammar (Brown & Hanlon)

➤ The View from Hypolingualism (Stromswold)

B. Some Examples

➤ Motherese?

*(Interview by anthropologist Shirley Brice Heath with
"Aunt Mae," an AAE-speaking woman in the South Carolina Piedmont:)*

Aunt Mae: "Now just how crazy is dat? White folks uh hear dey kids say sump'n, dey say it back to 'em, dey aks 'em 'gain and 'gain 'bout things, like they 'posed to be born knowin'."

➤ Adult-Child interactions in Samoa

➤ Parenting in the !Kung San culture of southern Africa

➤ Correction for grammar or content?

Child:	Mama isn't boy, he a girl.
Mother:	That's right!

Child:	Disney comes on Tuesday.
Mother:	No. Wednesday.

(Brown & Hanlon, 1973)

SECTION 8

EARLY MILESTONES OF ACQUISITION

➤ Naturalistic Observation —

➤ Habituation Studies —

➤ Categorical Perception in Neonates —

➤ Phonetic Discrimination in Neonates —

➤ Babbling —

➤ Varied Babbling —

➤ Vocal Babbling in the Deaf —

➤ Restricted Phonetic Inventory —

SECTION 9

LATER MILESTONES

➤ Holophrastic Speech —

➤ Telegraphic Speech —

➤ Computational Bottleneck —

➤ The Vocabulary Explosion —

➤ Mean Length of Utterance (MLU) —

➤ The Grammar Explosion —

➤ Overregularization Errors —

➤ Metalinguistic Awareness —

1. Uniformity of language acquisition refers to the fact that:
    a. Language acquisition is uniformly slow.
    b. Language acquisition is uniformly easy and successful.
    c. Children are uniformly better at learning language than at learning math.

2. Holophrastic speech refers to the stage of language acquisition:
    a. when a child's utterances are three-dimensional.
    b. when a child uses two-word utterances but no function words.
    c. when a child uses single-word utterances.

3. In the course of childhood, sensitivity to differences in the sounds of the world's various languages:
    a. increases over time.
    b. decreases over time.
    c. stays the same over time.

4. The "Grammar Explosion" refers to a point in language development when:
    a. the child is overwhelmed by the volume of linguistic input.
    b. the child begins to use two-word utterances.
    c. the child suddenly starts to use function words.

UNIT III

BIOLOGICAL AND COMPUTATIONAL PERSPECTIVES ON LANGUAGE

SECTION 10

CEREBRAL LOCALIZATION

I. Coarse Anatomy of the Human Brain

Sketch an outline of the brain, and indicate where each area is located:

➤ Brain Stem

➤ Hypothalamus

➤ Thalamus

➤ Cerebellum

➤ Frontal Lobe

➤ Temporal Lobe

➤ Parietal Lobe

➤ Occipital Lobe

➤ Sylvian Fissure

➤ Perisylvian Region

II. Localization of Function:

Be prepared to indicate the area(s) of the cortex in which each function is localized:

➤ Motor Control

➤ Hearing

➤ Vision

➤ Spatial Reasoning

➤ Vocabulary

➤ Grammar

Be prepared to explain each of the following key terms:

➤ <u>Lateralization</u> of Language Function

➤ Plasticity in Childhood

Be prepared to describe the symptoms associated with each of these types of aphasia:

➤ Broca's Aphasia

➤ Isolation Aphasia

SECTION 11

CRITICAL PERIOD EFFECTS

➤ Critical Periods:

➤ Binocular Vision (in humans and certain other species)

➤ Language

➤ Language-learning by Adults:

➤ Incomplete Mastery of Tacit Rules

➤ Foreign Accents

SECTION 12

COMMUNICATION IN NON-HUMAN ANIMALS

"Language-Like" Abilities of Non-Human Species

A. Points of similarity between humans and (certain) other species:

➤ Communication with <u>conspecifics</u> through acoustic, visual, and other signals

➤ Capacity for Categorical Perception

➤ Capacity for Word-recognition

➤ Capacity to associate words with behaviors (e.g. in dogs)

➤ Capacity to associate visual stimuli with words (e.g. in parrots)

B. Points unique (so far as we know) to humans:

➤ Rapid, internally driven acquisition of new word-meaning pairs

➤ The Creative Aspect of Human Language:

    ➤ <u>Rule-governed combination</u> of parts to create novel expressions

    ➤ <u>Rule-governed analysis</u> for comprehension of novel expressions

SECTION 13

THE COMPUTER METAPHOR FOR HUMAN COGNITION

Be prepared to explain each of the following key terms:

➤ Automaton —

➤ Cognitive Psychology —

➤ Generative Grammar —

➤ Formal Languages —

➤ Natural Languages —

➤ Syntax —

➤ Semantics —

➤ Decision Procedure —

➤ Phrase Structure Grammar —

SECTION 14

NATURAL LANGUAGE AND ARTIFICIAL INTELLIGENCE

➤ Artificial Intelligence

➤ Natural Language Processing

➤ Machine Translation

Examples of machine translation (1998, AltaVista's automatic translation service, using SysTran):

1. a. The book about the invention of the telephone is on the shelf.
   b. Le livre concernant l'invention du téléphone est sur l'étagère.
   c. The book concerning the invention of the telephone is on the rack.

2. a. Visiting relatives can be boring.
   b. Les parents visitants peuvent être ennuyeux.
   c. The visiting parents can be tedious.

3. a. The claims held up to careful scrutiny.
   b. Les réclamations retardées à l'examen minutieux soigneux.
   c. Complaints delayed with the careful meticulous examination.

Fragment of a simple PSG for English:

- ➤ R1: S → NP_sg AUX_sg PP | NP_pl AUX_pl PP

- ➤ R2: NP_sg → Det N_sg (PP)

- ➤ R3: NP_pl → Det N_pl (PP)

- ➤ R4: N_sg → book | invention | telephone | shelf

- ➤ R5: N_pl → books

- ➤ R6: AUX_sg → is

- ➤ R7: AUX_pl → are

- ➤ R8: PP → P NP_sg | P NP_pl

- ➤ R9: Det → the

- ➤ R10: P → on | about | of

1. Language processing occurs mainly in the ___ lobes of the brain.
   a. occipital and parietal
   b. parietal and temporal
   c. frontal and temporal

2. Visual processing occurs mainly in the ___ lobe of the brain.
   a. frontal
   b. temporal
   c. occipital

3. A patient with Broca's Aphasia usually:
   a. speaks fluently, but makes no sense.
   b. has perfect control of grammar, but omits content words.
   c. understands content words, but has impaired grammatical abilities.

4. The critical period for language acquisition refers to:
   a. the period when a child becomes critical of the parents' language.
   b. the period when a child can acquire a language without having a foreign accent.
   c. the period when the child's brain achieves critical mass.

5. Attempts to teach human language to chimpanzees have been most successful in:
   a. syntax.
   b. vocabulary.
   c. speech.

Unit IV

Phrase Structure

Section 15

The Structure of Declarative Sentences

- ➤ PS Rules

- ➤ PS Trees / Tree Diagrams / Phrase Markers

- ➤ Root Node

- ➤ Branches

- ➤ Intermediate Nodes

- ➤ Terminal Nodes

- ➤ Terminal Elements

- ➤ Mother → Daughter Daughter

```
        Mother
         / \
Daughter   Daughter
```

➤ Root Node of a Simple Declarative Sentence: IP

➤ Basic PS Rules for English:

IP → NP I'   VP → V'
I' → I VP   V' → V (NP)

NP → (Det) N'   PP → P'
N' → N (PP)   P' → P NP

➤ Descriptive Adequacy

➤ Undergeneration

➤ Overgeneration

➤ Syntax

➤ Semantics

➤ Specifiers across Categories:

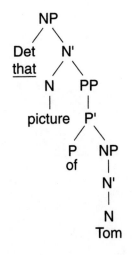

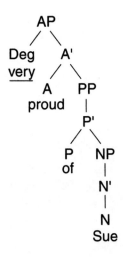

```
         PP
        /  \
     Deg    P'
    well   /  \
          P    NP
        above   |
                N'
                |
                N
              average
```

```
         XP
        /  \
 (Specifier)  X'
             /  \
            X  (Complement)
```

➤ The X-Bar Schema:

XP → (Specifier) X'
X' → X (Complement)

where X $\in$ {N, A, V, P, I}

➤ Simple sentence = IP, where I $\in$ {PRES, PAST, will, might, must, ...} .

SECTION 17

X-BAR PARAMETERS

The X-Bar __Principles__:

$XP \rightarrow X'$ (Specifier) \\
$X' \rightarrow X$ (Complement) |- __Left-to-right order may vary.__
$X' \rightarrow X' ZP$ /

where X, Z $\in$ {N, A, V, P, I}

The X-Bar __Parameters__:

__Specifiers__ appear to the {left, right} of X'.

__Complements__ appear to the {left, right} of X.

English: __Specifiers__ to the __left__;
  __Complements__ to the __right__.

```
              XP
             /  \
    (Specifier)   X'
                 /  \
                X  (Complement)
```

Japanese: Specifiers to the left;
            Complements to the left.

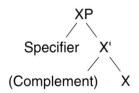

XP
Specifier   X'
(Complement)   X

(Revised) X-Bar Schema for English:

XP → (Specifier) X'
X' → X (Complement)

where X $\in$ {N, A, V, P, I, <u>C</u>}

V: *think, ask, wonder, ...*
C (= <u>Complementizer</u>): *that, whether, if*

> [$_{IP}$ John thinks <u>that</u> [$_{IP}$ Mary saw Fred]]

(Question: What word order do we expect in the Japanese translation?)

Recursion within the X-Bar Schema helps account for the <u>creativity</u> of language.

1. In the phrase "the book about linguistics", which of the following is a terminal element?
   a. NP
   b. N'
   c. book

2. In the phrase "the book about linguistics", which of the following is a specifier?
   a. the
   b. book
   c. linguistics

3. Which of the following is the X-bar structure for a phrase in English?

   a.
   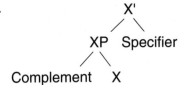

   b.
   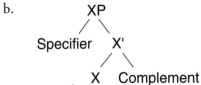

   c.
   Complement
      /   \
   X'   XP
   / \   /   \
  X   X   Specifier

4. A major difference between English and Japanese is that:
   a. In Japanese, a specifier appears to the left of X'.
   b. In Japanese, a complement appears to the left of X.
   c. In Japanese, a specifier appears to the right of X'

Unit V

Transformations

Section 19

Head Movement

I. Complementizer Phrases (CP's)

John thinks [$_{CP}$ <u>that</u> Sue will win]

```
                        IP
                      /    \
                   NP        I'
                   |        /  \
                   N'     I      VP
                   |   (PRES)    |
                   N             V'
                  John          /  \
                              V      CP
                            think    |
                                     C'
                                   /   \
                                 C       IP
                               that    /   \
                                     NP      I'
                                     |      / \
                                     N'    I    VP
                                     |   will   |
                                     N          V'
                                    Sue         |
                                                V
                                               win
```

II. I-to-C Movement

A. Root Node for Interrogative Sentences = **CP**

B. **I-to-C Movement:** If the entire sentence is interrogative (e.g., a *yes/no*-question), move the contents of the <u>matrix</u> I into C.

D-Structure

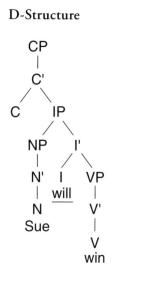

S-Structure

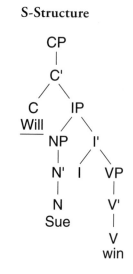

50

SECTION 20

PHRASAL MOVEMENT

I. Movement Rules (or "Transformations")

I-to-C Movement: If the entire sentence is interrogative (i.e., a *yes/no*-question or *wh*-question), move the contents of the <u>matrix</u> I into C.

Wh-movement: Move an NP with the [+wh] feature into the specifier position of CP, and leave a <u>trace</u> (t) in the NP's previous position.

II. Indirect Wh-questions

John asked [$_{CP}$ ___ (C) [$_{IP}$ Fred will drink <u>what</u>]]   D-Structure

↓ *Wh-Movement*

John asked [$_{CP}$ <u>what</u> (C) [$_{IP}$ Fred will drink <u>t</u>]]   S-Structure

III. Direct Wh-questions

[$_{CP}$ ___ (C) [$_{IP}$ Fred **will** drink <u>what</u>]]   D-Structure

↓ *I-to-C Movement*

[$_{CP}$ ___ **will** [$_{IP}$ Fred **(I)** drink <u>what</u>]]   (Intermediate Structure)

↓ *Wh-Movement*

[$_{CP}$ <u>What</u> will [$_{IP}$ Fred **(I)** drink <u>t</u>]]   S-Structure

IV. Successive Cyclic Movement

$[_{CP}$ ___ (C) John **will** think $[_{CP}$ ___ (C) $[_{IP}$ Fred could find <u>what</u>]]]   **D-Structure**

↓   *Wh-Movement*

$[_{CP}$ ___ (C) John **will** think $[_{CP}$ <u>what</u> (C) $[_{IP}$ Fred could find <u>t</u>]]]   (Intermediate Structure)

↓   *I-to-C Movement*

$[_{CP}$ ___ **will** John (I) think $[_{CP}$ <u>what</u> (C) $[_{IP}$ Fred could find <u>t</u>]]]   (Intermediate Structure)

↓   *Wh-Movement*

$[_{CP}$ <u>What</u> **will** John (I) think $[_{CP}$ <u>t</u> (C) $[_{IP}$ Fred could find <u>t</u>]]]   **S-Structure**

SECTION 21

WH ERRORS IN CHILDREN LEARNING ENGLISH

I. Successive-cyclic movement

$[_{CP}$ ___ (C) John **will** think $[_{CP}$ ___ (C) $[_{IP}$ Fred could find <u>what</u> $]]]$ **D-Structure**

↓ *Wh-Movement*

$[_{CP}$ ___ (C) John **will** think $[_{CP}$ <u>what</u> (C) $[_{IP}$ Fred could find <u>t</u> $]]]$ (Intermediate Structure)

↓ *I-to-C Movement*

$[_{CP}$ ___ **will** John (I) think $[_{CP}$ <u>what</u> (C) $[_{IP}$ Fred could find <u>t</u> $]]]$ (Intermediate Structure)

↓ *Wh-Movement*

$[_{CP}$ <u>What</u> **will** John (I) think $[_{CP}$ <u>t</u> (C) $[_{IP}$ Fred could find <u>t</u> $]]]$ **S-Structure**

II. A parameter of *wh*-movement

The "Medial Wh" Parameter: The trace of long-distance *wh*-movement that is left in an intermediate specifier-of-CP position {**can, cannot**} be pronounced.

English: <u>cannot</u>

5. **What** do you think $[_{CP} \mathbf{t_{NP}}$ C $[_{IP}$ John bought $\mathbf{t_{NP}}]]$?

6. * **What** do you think $[_{CP}$ **what** C $[_{IP}$ John bought $\mathbf{t_{NP}}]]$?

German (Southern Dialects): <u>can</u>

7. **Was** glaubst du $[_{CP} \mathbf{t_{NP}}$ dass $[_{IP}$ Hans $\mathbf{t_{NP}}$ gekauft hat $]]$?
   what believe you $[_{CP} \mathbf{t_{NP}}$ that $[_{IP}$ John $\mathbf{t_{NP}}$ bought has$]]$?
   'What do you think that John bought?'

8. **Was** glaubst du $[_{CP}$ **was** $[_{IP}$ Hans $\mathbf{t_{NP}}$ gekauft hat $]]$?
   what believe you $[_{CP} (\mathbf{t_{NP}})$ $[_{IP}$ John $\mathbf{t_{NP}}$ bought has$]]$?
   'What do you think that John bought?'
   [more literally, '<u>What</u> do you think <u>what</u> John bought?']

III. Children's errors during the acquisition of wh-movement

Medial-*wh* questions in children's English: (Thornton 1990, McDaniel 1989)

10.   **What** do you think [$_{CP}$ **what** C [$_{IP}$ Cookie Monster eats t_{NP}]] ?

Observation: Children's "errors" in *wh*-movement are sometimes grammatical in other languages.

Implication: Children are born with a limited range of parametric options, and errors in the course of language acquisition may take the form of choosing incorrectly among these options.

SECTION 22

WANNA CONTRACTION

I. Silent NPs ("Empty Categories")

Current syntactic theory recognizes at least two types of silent (unpronounced) NPs:

Trace: NP   (Traces result from movement transformations.)
                |
                t

PRO: NP   (PRO = silent pronoun)
                |
             PRO

In English, PRO often serves as the subject of an infinitive clause.

John wants [$_{IP}$ Mary to leave].
John wants [$_{IP}$ PRO to leave].   [PRO refers back to John.]

II. *Wanna* Contraction Revisited

want + to → *wanna*

The process of *wanna* contraction is constrained for many (though not all) English speakers:

When pronouncing the S-Structure tree, *want + to* can be pronounced as *wanna*, so long as there is no intervening <u>trace in Specifier of IP</u>.

(An intervening <u>trace in Specifier of CP</u> does not matter, nor does an intervening <u>PRO</u>.)

Who could she want to visit?   (Answer: She could want to visit Mary.)
Who could she wanna visit?   (Answer: She could wanna visit Mary.)

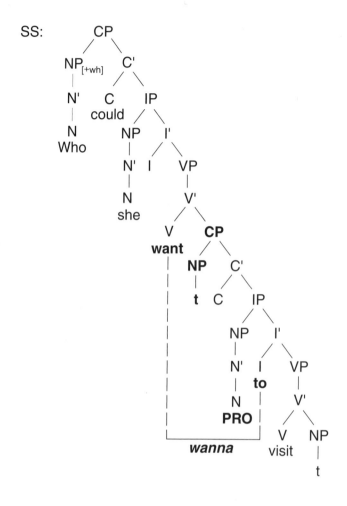

Who could she want to visit Mary?   (Answer: She could want Fred to visit Mary.)
*Who could she wanna visit Mary?

SS:

CP
NP[+wh]   C'
N'   C   IP
could
N   NP   I'
Who
N'   I   VP
she
V'
V   CP
want
NP   C'
t   C   **IP**
NP   I'
t   I   VP
to
V'
* wanna
V   NP
visit
N'
N
Mary

57

III. Do preschool children know the constraints on *wanna* contraction in English?

Studies of children's spontaneous speech: Hard to tell.

Studies of elicited speech: Children overwhelmingly obey the constraints.

Thornton (1990):

Experimenter:	Ratty looks hungry. I bet he wants to eat something. Ask Ratty what he wants.
Child:	What do you <u>want to / wanna</u> eat? [Contraction more than 85% of the time]
Experimenter:	Ok, there are three guys in this story: Cookie Monster, a dog, and this baby. One of them gets to take a walk, one gets to take a nap, and one gets to eat a cookie. And the rat gets to choose who does each thing. So, one gets to take a walk, right? Ask Ratty who he wants.
Child:	Who do you <u>want to / * wanna</u> take a walk? [Contraction less than 10% of the time]

Section 23

Structure Dependence in Child Language

I-to-C Movement: If the entire sentence is interrogative, move the contents of the <u>matrix</u> I into C.

Crain & Nakayama (1987). Thirty three- to five-year-old children.

Experimenter: Ask Jabba if [the man who is beating a donkey] is mean.

Child: Is [the man who is beating a donkey] __ mean?

[Typical response]

Child: * Is [the man who __ beating a donkey] is mean?

[0% of responses]

1. In which of the following has I-to-C Movement applied?
   a. Is Mary happy?
   b. Mary is happy.
   c. I wonder if Mary is happy.

2. The D-Structure for the question "Is Mary happy?" is:

   a.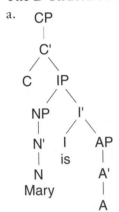

   b.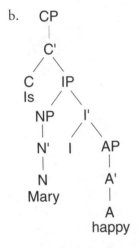

   c.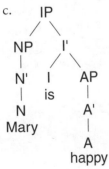

3. Which of the following sentences has identical D-Structure and S-Structure?
   a. Can John see Mary?
   b. John can see Mary.
   c. Who can see Mary?

4. What transformational rule applies in the derivation for "The student will know who Mary might like"?
   a. I-to-C movement
   b. *Wh*-movement
   c. The student-rights movement

5. *Wanna* contraction is blocked by:
   a. a PRO in the Specifier of IP.
   b. a trace in the Specifier of IP.
   c. a trace in the Specifier of CP.

6. The best method for studying children's knowledge of *wanna* contraction is:
   a. naturalistic observation.
   b. elicited production.
   c. the habituation technique.

Unit VI

Language in Exceptional Circumstances

Section 24

Language in the Visual Modality

I. Signed Languages of the Deaf

ASL, LSQ, BSL, ISN, etc.

II. American Sign Language (ASL)

Lexicon of abstract symbols (words), with *limited* iconicity

Grammatical structure

UG Constraints

Wh-movement cannot cross a filled Specifier-of-CP position

Parameter-settings permitted by UG

Null Arguments

Optionality of *Wh*-movement

III. Acquisition of ASL

Acquired as a native language (by deaf children of deaf adults)

Stages of acquisition are similar to those for an auditory language.

Babbling (first vocal and then gestural), one-word stage, first two-word combinations, grammar explosion, etc.

Critical period effects

Acquisition by young children is rapid, seemingly effortless, and relatively error-free.

Acquisition by adults is laborious, and permanently marked by a "foreign accent."

IV. Aphasia

Aphasic syndromes exist for signed languages, and closely parallel those for auditory languages.

Section 25

Pidgins and Creoles

Key Terms:

➤ Pidgin—

➤ Substrate Languages—

➤ Superstrate Language—

➤ Lexifier Language—

➤ Creole—

Case Study: Hawaiian Pidgin English (HPE) and Hawaiian Creole English (HCE)

Example of HPE: (Bickerton 1981, p. 26)

      mi iste nalehu tu yia
      'I was in Nalehu for two years.'

Example of HCE: (Bickerton 1981, p.28)

      ai no kea hu stei hant insai dea, ai gon hunt
      'I don't care who's hunting in there, I'm going to hunt.'

Note the use of sentence embedding and the aspectual marker *stei*.

SECTION 26
THE BIRTH OF A NEW LANGUAGE

➤ Managua School for the Deaf (founded 1978)

Be prepared to give some characteristics of each of the following:

➤ Home Sign

➤ Lenguaje de Signos Nicaragüense (LSN)

➤ Idioma de Signos Nicaragüense (ISN, Nicaraguan Sign Language)

1. Which of the following statements is true?
   a. Pidgins are based on European languages, and creoles are based on African languages.
   b. Pidgins have richer structure than creoles.
   c. Pidgins are nobody's mother tongue, while creoles are acquired as a first language.

2. Which of the following statements is true?
   a. All deaf people across the world use the same sign language.
   b. Sign languages are grammatically more primitive than spoken languages.
   c. Sign languages and spoken languages are based on the same universal principles.